W9-BMA-500

thieves' latin

WINNER OF THE IOWA POETRY PRIZE

poems by **peter jay shippy**

thieves' latin

UNIVERSITY OF IOWA PRESS Ψ *Iowa City*

University of Iowa Press, Iowa City 52242

Copyright © 2003 by Peter Jay Shippy

Printed in the United States of America

Design by Richard Hendel

http://www.uiowa.edu/uiowapress

The publication of this book was generously supported
by the University of Iowa Foundation.

Printed on acid-free paper

Library of Congress Cataloging-in-Publication Data
Shippy, Peter Jay, 1961–
    Thieves' Latin: poems / by Peter Jay Shippy.
        p.   cm.–(The Iowa poetry prize)
    ISBN 0-87745-840-5 (paper)
        I. Title.   II. Series.
PS3619.H58 T48 2003
811'.6–dc21   2002075076

03 04 05 06 07 P 5 4 3 2 1

for

Nancy & Harold,

my mother & father

Contents

PART THREE

Acknowledgments

CrossConnect: "Inhaler."

Denver Quarterly: "Buzzcocked" and "*Sehnsucht.*"

Epoch: "Earth Is a Lonely Town."

Expressions: "Little Poe Station."

Five A.M.: "The Skidding of Tottie Coughdrop."

Harvard Review: "Not the Kind of Poem Found in the Japanese Edition of Tiger Beat or the Ballad of the Bodiless Man."

Ploughshares: "Ether Talk" and "Me My Dog and Our Pornography."

Poetry Ireland: "Crocodiles Shed Their Tears When Devouring Francis Bacon," "No One Understands Who I Really Am So I Will Wear Copper Cladding, Oxidize, Turn Green and Blend in with the Trees," and "The Bowling Pin Forest."

slope.org: "Dogs Resembling Their Owners," "Fink," "Niagara, Niagara," and "Portrait of God on Work Release."

I would like to thank the Massachusetts Cultural Council for their generous grant.

thieves' latin

America, USA

No, there were no artists in the family. I guess my mother encouraged
my art. My father didn't, he was a practical person. Like too practical. When
I decided to go to art school he didn't totally approve of that because it
didn't promise his son a living. It seemed too far-fetched to him, not utilitarian
enough. So he wanted me to be anything but an artist. So when I went to art
school he supported me for the first couple of years I was there. Then in *Post*
magazine—which was a very popular magazine in the States at that time, in
the mid '50s—he saw an article on Walt Disney. Of course, he knew who
Walt Disney was, but he didn't know that Walt supported our school. When
he found out, all ideas changed. He liked the idea that his son would go to a
school supported by Walt Disney.—Ed Ruscha

I dig mixing—I don't grind—can't tag me—
    in the morning I wipe the bark
        from my eyes—

I pick the purlieu off my shadows
    and shake away the idylls—
        when my eyes

become alarmingly clear I can see
    so much work to do—so sleep falls
        back to me.

one

The Special People

When the special people came they put us off pills. They made
us swallow our work. Those showed us ways to conjugate
our wounds. When the special people came they spotted for us.
We ran fast when they told us *run*. We sang loud when they said
stitch in time. Or, *not forever*. Or, *swing low*. Or, *am a fate*.

When the special people came they put us indoors. They had
us embellish our lyrics. Those showed us ways to leave out
for birds. When the special people came they deleted for us.
We watched when they said look. We sang loud when they said
tongue in cheek. And, *pitch shifter*. And, *piss off*. Or, *go cat go*.

A ghost by everything is still a ghost. A tolerable penny is one
found heads up. A man and his secret reunite in a western desert.
The people wait us on that old front porch. Those spare us
all the messy detachments. Life is what you get away with.

Crocodiles Shed Their Tears
When Devouring Francis Bacon

It was the summer we dosed with coffin cider
        and sipped cold tear soup to starch-up our shadows.

I kept darning spiders in my old sock drawer
        and wore a plain locket that held a pike's tooth.

Down off Eel Road, time boned into a lovely lea
        of bee balm and indigo. I often picnicked there.

Hummingbirds sprung from phlox to phlox as I read
        Chandlers. Crime organized. Wan asterisks buzzed.

At dusk, I often napped to the electric razors
        that hotly chirruped like Ma's hairy cicadas.

A grand singing turtle took her season's residence
        in the new pear orchard. I think she ate well.

It was in late August that I opened the matchbox
        to set a wing of positrons loose. Does it matter?

That slim season went south when I found out
        that the dueling crickets had rigged their bouts.

Why Is the Crow a Harmful Bird?

You have a good feeling about most birds, and trust
that they are a friend to man. Canaries arrive by
the bucketful for the holiday trade in America. Geese
can sense the magnetic fields that surround our planet.
Most accept a theory of evolution, but those that don't
have a notion that explains how birds came to be—
time travel. We can go over each part of the body
of a bird and find traces of the future. Certain glands
in birds secrete nanobots that produce tiny black holes.
Birds say that millennia from now wings will be used
for touristic rituals. Their eyes are image orthicons.
Why do our birds migrate across time's dank artery?
No one knows. No one. A mockingbird was once heard
to mimic the notes of 32 different birds in 10 minutes
using a chip embedded in its false beak. A little known
fact about parrots is that when crapulent, they are brave
and loyal. Green parrots will train on the Arizona coast.
The African gray parrot believes that a human's shadow
is part of its soul or *ignis fatuus*, foolish fire. No bird has
been written about so much by poets as the nightingale.
The attempt to download its odes goes back to Sappho.
In the frozen arctic districts owls have snowy plumage
and Kevlar flaps over their ears, to avoid God's call.
Toucans are sometimes visible. The stormy petrel only
sings in Pidgin English. There are many reasons why
it may be necessary to pass laws to protect the emperor
penguin from nuclear attack, one reason, strangely enough,
is that this penguin has few, if any, enemies. Not crows.

A crow once plucked my child right from under my nose.
In World War III crows will be dropped in large numbers.
The air over cities will resemble the feather of a church fire.
When the crow is sky I will hear my dear's hoarse cry.
I am building bamboo wings. No one knows. No one.

Stars by Children

The last ferry departs the station in October. You
read the instructions creasing her forehead, her
eyes fold like little brains in mint formaldehyde.
Most of the village will jump into the final boat.
It's tradition. It's palpable. They have palm pilots
and maps inset with emblems of the present unease.
The night before the exit there is a coffee klatch
in the banquet hall of the volunteer fire department.
You plan to attend. You walk. The street is wound
with dark seaweed, oak leaves and fishing cable.
The moon is in pratfall, light escaping its reliquary.
A barn owl sits a staff of trembling branches. It
looks like a hex note carved into a folk song;
its electric cowl suckers a rat. Feel a pinch in
the webbing between two toes? You're hooked.

Hours later, at the end of that line—the old men.
God dies, we fish as always, one says, pulling his
star out of your skin. Their trawlers tinkle like
stained shards from the Cathedral of Blue Crane.
She said, please be careful please be wise, please—
I don't want to have your child. The others nod.
They hand you a mug of thick soup. It smells like
a muddy pond and plants in you a yen to smoke.
The doorknobs in my bedroom grow hot near
midnight, charged as they are with premonitions.
You offer your pack around. *Your problem is*
teaching your cats to walk upright. You can stand
this pause forever. They give you a soft pear.

Someone starts a fire in an oil drum. A siren
from the other side of your island elicits giggles.

She meets you for a beer at the Sirius. The air
doesn't take to your lungs. Noise approaching
speech leaks out a titanium radio transistor behind
the counter. Thumbnail size Christmas lights
are strung from the cherry beams like swamp gas.
I feel like we're inside an abandoned submarine
she says. You want to pull at her sutures to see
if that will make another voice take over speaking.
Would you like to dance? You would. She and you
flutter across the peeling linoleum like late asters.
She presses your face into her soft neck like a dead
man into the mask's wax mold. This is preterition.
A kind soul plays you loud music to hide inside.
Her brown hair in your mouth reminds you that
it will snow soon. *Tomorrow I'm already gone.*

After the bar you buy a bottle to walk the island.
Fruit bats track moths with ultrasonic pulses. You
nod. This passes for talk. You point up, past
the sugar maple's totemic delta. The sky is that
black that allows blue to believe it is not a color.
The sky glowers like Gainsborough's faces.
Vertigo is the mischief of the waltz. In 1801
the vulgar whirling caused hundreds of stillbirths.
Next season, the Austrian tuber crop went south.
Your walking stirs the metal insects that live near
the Marine Research Center. This is where to catch
a priest matching lures with hatching mayflies.
Victory creepers raise their stalkheads like mikes.
She sings a snatch of Bernoulli's law of large numbers.
Consider the life without departures. All at twice.

As you cross a plowed orchard your feet sink, as
in orthopedics. She stops for a salt popper. You
put your hands across your chest as in opera love.
She scales sand. *I can see that church. Let's go.*
When she slides down the other side of the dune,
there is that feeling—nothing watches you. All at
once. No one is studying you or keeping score or
believing in you. This has its ups and its downs.
Where is that noise like the wind through bone
ash that eliminates all other sounds? You turn
back to the village, the blurred trace of impression
remakes itself like a skeleton with glue and skin.
From the east a slim yawn of light provides grace.
You remember a thing she said, *If I kiss you now
my eyes might roll around. I could fall. Okay?*

Fireflies scatter at your step like cheap buckshot.
Remember when you still could travel, you were
north near the Arctic Circle, Europe. You were
eating venison in a hotel restaurant while reading
The Loneliness of the Long Player Turntablist.
You sipped peach vodka. There was a soft party
in a corner whose children chanted your name.
How? Was this prophecy or just happenstance?
You used a pocket translator that spoke robot—
the voice of tomorrow—to ask your waitress (so
wrinkled she looked like a baby): What lives?
I the butt of hospitality? She laughed, said, *No,
your name is our word for broken eggs. Just that.
Drink up. Eat on.* When she told the party they
turned and blew you tears. They sent chocolate.

You catch up to her at Juniper Cove, she stares at
the sea's melisma. The sun runs slower uphill than

down, but there's enough dawn for the dumb show.
A hawk feigns death and dives into the star garden.
Sere flickers sing like worn squeeze toys. Last July
she mistook a bat slick for clouds of smoke. She
thought the Village was on fire. Hatch of flies.
Knot of snake. Steam of minnows. She and you:
right here, skin on her belly as hot as summer glass.
Her tongue set the pendulum of your cortex to numb.
From the Blue Crane's steeple you hear PowerBooks
and Nord Modulars deliver Björk's Psalm 21.
Biologists can prove that this stunts sour myrtle.
A brood of wasps. A Bolshevik of ant. Murmur
of starlings. The Perseids lost to the corn moon.

On the beach you sit and rest. She eats rice cakes
topped with Bengal honey. You finish the bottle.
You take out a pen and a card: RAY'S RAYS.
The sky (a *trompe l'oeil?*) is medulla oblongata.
The day breaks everywhere twice. You watch
Foxgloves groove across the sky, their feathers
are beautifully botched, like a child's rendering
of Christ. *The kind of day to listen to the Sox or
think about Rimbaud returning to France to die.*
Like a dream of A.M. scream gems, a creature
walks from the ocean toward you. It's a man in
a wet suit. He takes off his mask, shilly-shally
clings to his seal skin. He's a scientist slash priest,
studying far-eyed tortoises. He's seven feet tall.
He says: You have hours before the ferry leaves.

The Cathedral of Blue Crane squats on a bluff
above Quarantine Harbor and the lost hamlet.
From a ship it resembles a petrified glass mantis.

Over black tea and Gyoza dumplings the Father
says: My kind is being swapped for small ones,
your size, aesthetics matched to glitch science, it
makes the world grow. A brass green tortoise
rolls a Croquet ball across a manicured lawn.
A box trap behind the outdoors-confessional snaps.
He says: Another wrinkled shadow on the wall,
hell, brother, we're either *sine qua non* or not
and both mean nothing. Wires hum. Oaks shake
like wet dogs. On the floor with the other jaws
Nature, expansive by nature, shrinks to include
you. Take it. The stars in your tea start to dance.

Here, the sea is freckled with glow sirens. Their
song is looped, a generative system. They smell
rain. As you rise you overturn a beggar's bowl
of gooseberries floating in chocolate milk. He
says: Our strand does not stand for evanescence,
it's sand for the sake of sand, pure and free from
debate on sand; sit in the lifeguard's nest; our sand
is a meditation on sand, stuff your ears with fingers
and hear the sea taking her away, the ferry is gone,
take your pen, write—*What's not here I will send
in a bottle with the next sleeper walking your way.*
Click. In the Sirius your wrinkles whir, Slav voices
sing, *Be-Bop-A-Lu-La.* Imagine a deft surgeon
painting a dotted line across your apple. You feel
nothing but articulation. And I don't mean maybe.

When Alice Coltrane Calls

A building resembles a raincoat. The night sky is shutter
clicked. The darkroom conditions of the dance floor allow
me to take advantage of foreshadowing. She refuses to join
the rest of us on our US tour on the grounds that America
doesn't exist. Flash, hush. When Alice Coltrane calls it
is lissome like the air between mortars or that sweet way
Wittgenstein recited mantra and raga on "The Firebird."
Some winter sparrows wear raincoats. The strobes cut
away the icicles hanging like thumbs off my blue arms.
The woman who inhales inexorables licks my lips, stirs
my drink. When I lived in Spain, she says, I was moved
by an unseen hand, she says, I would witness the reverse
side of actions, she says, before the verse side could occur,
she says, as if my trips have any interest for you, or me.
Wearing a coat that resembles a Philip Johnson, I hear
fire humming. On stage, a cellist lights a match and waits
for it to go out. But her old gang, an internationally in-
famous 4-tet has booby-trapped her illuminator. Now
she's unable to move beyond transcription. They place
her in the straitjacket of interpretation. Watch us fall.
There's a gray cat in the corner kinking her strings like
hawthorn roots, like iris, like when Alice Coltrane calls.

Transgenic Laureate

London

Everyone is someone or knows someone or has just been
someone in a film or play or commercial or Maoist ballet.
The air is so thick with chest-beating and existential smoke
that the gallery goes Delphic. The future rolls up her sleeves.

Someone from Tussaud's Q-tips my mouth, mining DNA.

Berlin

When our stark taxi ran over the column of ash lining
the Tiergarten's dermal edges, I was hurled into the eternal
reconstruction zone surrounding Potsdamer Platz. The driver
appears to be life challenged. Now, I feel distinctly now.

The Idiot plays as my eyes stammer, all *succès de scandale.*

Boston

I have yet to hear from them so this is Chinese whispers, not
from them personally, so if it's just rumors—hey—I say so.
But you know what they say? If Hong Kong whispers the world
buys Japanese hearing aids. The future is distinctly now.

Someone from Tussaud's arrives to apply my dayglow.

Ether Talk

Photo of Beckett on the fridge.

> He and I, smoke.

All three of us are humming.

> A gust twitches

the kitchen window's plastic wedge.

> I see a neighbor

at tai chi, posing like a Giacometti.

> Two sides of a piece.

Every shape is a way out.

From down the block we

> hear teen tuneage:

Bad bad fucking very bad.

> Autumn: winter

exudes the air. I boil water.

> The thing to do.

Autumn: maker of ghost.

> Moon loser.

Sam puffs.

> I light one, too.

With all this elongation I don't wish to appear rude.

Two Stans Eat

The graviotensile dials
   on the dashboard panel

resemble a snow owl
   squashed by a steamroller.

The disc rack is acid
   green polyethylene.

Our Yamamoto clothes
   suggest undersea writhing.

We ate lunch from a glassbox
   and ogled fungi growing

al dente off the K-beams
   of the paperweight tower.

I wish I could tell you—

your eyes have elegies
   rare in pit-stop amenities—

   I just wish I could say.

M axEr nst

The child passes to sleep in the piano's chalk circle. The lake's bilious
spray gives avenue for the pike to leave the deeps. What in the end needs

to be shrunken (the face in the rice moon to a peony head) needs to be
pulled like a prank or a rug or that damn sweet third or hair or a punch.

When the great collagista was nine, a danger heron whispers this message
into the boy's pink cockle: *Where the mum is mum / the fair Gardener*

is perfuse. It is a matter of direct observation that the artist will not
know his subject until his life is almost over. Their meeting is a matter

of public record and private Zen — they lunch at Max's Kansas City.
The omniscient dogpa of final things is howling from that small stage.

When the boy stands up to his strain, a syntactic approach threatens
to destroy his cairn, made from: paper flowers, a Swiss bank, thread,

nods from the assassination racket, fish teeth, a lammergeier's feather,
a b/w ultravox, 100,000 doves, tack lines, tops, turned-up moustaches,

scarecrow straw, chocolate, coffee, tobacco, oil, salt and two comets.
Like a back room aviator he attaches our planet to the highest branch.

Under and under throughout his life life stains. The train's silhouette
races past as encaustic bees sidle like magnet shavings toward the sun.

Bunnyman, an Elegy

for Stephen

Once upon, it rained. I didn't see it start. That's sad as that's
the best part of a November storm. Yet, it was a wonderful day
from a week without presets. There are stranger elsewheres?
The clouds look dopey like summer sheep or helium balloons away
above the taut wires which are fences or strings. Here, things are
disappearing. An Arab strap, a book on amber insects, my favorite
pair of cords and a small figurine of Ganesh. The cat was absent
a whole day. But I believe that she was still here, just hiding.
Every void describes a world. Every void describes a word.
Somewhere in an elegy the odds must appear. Where are you
making away with our things? We joke about another dimension.
I have not mentioned your certain culpability. I'm not sure
of my wife's opinion on ghosts. A crow coughs the rotten ash.
The tree looks like a scroll dying to unroll and announce your
perfect attendance. I will never forget the day before we met.
What is vestigial can be measured. Levi. Leviathan. Levitation.
When it rains in winter the colors are simple, the horizon lines
are brittle. What more do you want? How long will it be before
I hear gems cracking and Neolithic crickets playing requiems?

And then one rainy day you need a person to read you a poem.

No One Understands Who I Really Am
So I Will Wear Copper Cladding, Oxidize,
Turn Green and Blend in with the Trees

I am tossed back into the kite-capped sea—
too small, that sick stink, and only four limbs.

I float on my back counting the star-dyed sheep
until I hitch a lift with a moon powered tug,

back toward land. I keep my heart buttoned
so as not to disturb the hourglass keeper.

On a sandbar, a tar sets me up and regales
with tales of Oedipus. "Not the one by Soph,"

he says, "the other one. The one who fails
the riddle and walks off to see the world.

He marries a girl his own age. They adopt.
See what I'm saying?" he asks. I bobble.

"Look over there," he says, pointing at
a rocky spit of land below Duino Castle.

There is a lone figure, a pensive serif
perched on a dolomite, lapping his Apple.

"That Rilke sits there all day, half the night,
waiting for perspiration. Let's give 'em an earful."

He takes out his brass megaphone and blows—
"If you scream your dandy head off, *who*

will hear you among the company of angels!"
Rainer begins to type. After a dozen rounds

of tequila moaners I call it a morning and row
to shore, hoping to hell that God has forgotten

me. Just in case, I borrow a starfish ray
and pin it to my wet lapel. Just in case.

Reykjavik

A capital city
(about the size

of East Kafka)
where frostbitten

skin and spa
steam make

the place look
hardly lived in.

Me My Dog and Our Pornography

Open-in-the-name-of-the-Law
                                        is spoken.
Ah, writ happens. Next comes

the necessitous fist-fist against
our wooden door. We are under
our Amish divan View-Mastering

The 120 Days of Sodom while
whistling hardcore gabba and
breakbeat techno versions of

"The Internationale."
                                        We rise,
our wrists and paws extended,

ready for the cuff, prepared to
submit our sins into authority

on account of sanctity and our
excellent memoir-worthy guilts.

What will Court TV make us?

Outside, sirens and flashing lights
repeat their grim pronouncement.

Inside, my dog stops, and twists
his face into the doubting tommys.

"Wasn't it that vespertine Augustine,
who asked,"
                        asks my dog,

"'Is your management style limiting
the business of your success?'"

"Wasn't it that ol' Manx Marx
who said, 'Fornicate the police!'

"And, wasn't it dear Jesus
                              Hisself
who promised, 'If the end of history

is teleological then I'll change
your sweet wine into whiskey.'

"So,"
          my dog concludes, "why
not leave us to us and ours to ours?"

I scratch his remaining ear and
a few dust motes fly like fleas
or like aspirants to a paradise.

Sir, I say, you are correct, sir
but the neighbors' porcine faces
pressed against the windows,

their shitake shaped ears plugged
into the ends of bugs,
                              their eyes in

keyholes, at cubbyholes and mice
nooks have called up a warrant in
the profane sense of the word, but

in the sacred sense of our world
let's chant:
                    chant, chant, chant.

Let's break open a twelve-pack
and drink a toast to us, Americans
by birth, barkers by choice.

                    "Lovely,"
Dog says, pointing, as our door opens,
as electric truncheons are raised,

as guns are aimed my dog points out
up where the leaves from a stand
of young oaks shake like pompons

a nanosecond before they explode
into the aristos of autumn.

The Skidding of Tottie Coughdrop

I walk the orchards. A winter fog loses my feet and the trunks
so the apple limbs look snowflake, Rorschach, like the Chinese
characters for: hope, love, swell times, Bruce Lee and Motherwell.
January is barge, a slow lave.

I'm standing point on a gondola
greasing the grand canal of the Martian capital—Ohville—the dim
sun grounds an easy line that I botch à la Buckner. Bruckner?
His Ninth?—that's expense-account music.

Sorry, I'm a-chatter.
I recall my grandfather, the orchardman, day before his death
reply to his doctor's request to perform just one more surgery—

I already got the hook I guess the line and sinker don't matter.

Dig *that* dark emperor. Don't you love the antique charm of us
the ticked-off, the visitors, the exiteers, the gone; going, going.

Flying on Instruments

There is so much hard to come. An April blizzard leaves us
all kinetic. The livid aisle is unendurable. White suggests
heavy sedation: the gauze from bottles of cobweb remover.
Always the sky. Always that sponge. It just looks like play.

Certain flakes twinkle like certain effigies. The blue quality
of the high air slurs the sound as in eloquent sparring. Now,
we are a kind of family, the kind that tosses out our spines
with each new chill. The dusk was contaminated; dawn is

deadpan, to accent its atomic wrecking ball. "Excavation
has rendered improbable the postmodern theory of a chasm
with mephitic vapors." Air this high has a special name?
The other passengers are putting up a drama. It looks like

The Mikado as script doctored by Mamet. In order to remain
blipfree I volunteer to paint the scenery and take up cigars.
I pray for midday, for the tinkle of the serving cart wheedling
our arteries. "Maybe it's our vices that will endear us to God?"

says the man who sits nearest me. I've warned the bastard.
Even here, miles above the planet, summer just beetles. We
move our Marxist into the empty hot-food closet. A few
of us teach the others how to play Chinese Kino. One night

I take a walk on the wing. My heels click over the titanium as
in safe cracking. Looking up it's easy to think, improbable
is not impossible. Looking down I see the undiminished waves
of vagabondage press the surface like vines guided by psalms.

Just before Halloween we have our first leaper. The only shock is that it took this long. Someone, who saw said, "She looked like a sliver of gilt from a Caravaggio folio, the kind you find in Brentano's." Later, near the tail flaps (the smoker's Elba)

a DNA copyright attorney tells me he witnessed, too. "You ever set fire to a moth, huh?" His face is elmer and freckled with pugilistic light from the fin strobes. "Sure you have, with a magnifying glass. That's how she fell, man. Like a wink."

In the winter the sky turns oyster. We are lugged above volcano fields. I stick my head out the window to catch flakes of ash on my tongue. They feel like skin and taste like apple. Like, "The aureoles of affliction!" we sing. I no longer desire love.

As the New Year passes, some practice writing resumes and taking hostile interviews. The smell of rotting leaves calls us to a utility closet where we find cases of dandelion wine. No one will confess that this answers a prayer, so we toss them from

our belly hatch. On Groundhog Day I note, with cosmic irony, that most of us now sleep 20 hours a day. I forget what dogs sound like. Instead of dancing Tuesdays, couples hold hands and step off or out or drop into or, well, they depart this. This?

There is so much hard to come. An April blizzard leaves us with mephitic vapors. Air this high is airless is the exosphere. I take a walk on the wing. My heels click over the titanium as in safe cracking. Looking up it's easy to think, improbable.

Weathercast

Where the ferns are orange and the trillium blue dead monarchs
will fertilize the sweet rocket.

When a hailer worries your ear, ravens are speaking mouse.

Where a lunker bullfrog harps the last dither, a pogonip
will pluck a pine crystal to needle.

When Jesus was taken to air, his kneaded bread into birds.

Where speckled eggs nest in hawthorn, pause to parse
a rain skys plum wine.

Life breaks to say it.
                    Coo.

two

Was Postmodern

Her hair cops through my lips like a thread of fiber optics.

Ack-Ack

The soft evidence experts will aver

                that Shippy was not an epicure

of the first order. Normal wastes for

             a man of his posit and ambit:

a pack of smoke, this cryptic note,

           balls of twine inside a pine chest,

apple leaves, boughs, trunk embers

          groaning across the wheat without,

tin robots, Easter grass, glass tooth,

         a neo-Victorian oriole typewriter,

the 1938 film-noir classic, *Ack-Ack*

        on the Zenith in a constant loop,

a Mosler, a book, cough drops and one magnum of Childe in Amber.

The office near the empty safe offers

        little evidence for this case.

No blotches on his silk pjs or

       continents of sperm on his shag.

The kids in the lab will identify

        the ephebes under his bitten nails.

The Leader will set posses to the

       spew—sucked into plastic Baggies.

The Team's tasking—test, search,

interview—will fail to find the man,

his absence is as Klean™ as a

G-Man's serum. Alas. Alack:

a Sienese proverb: *After the meal wing and prawn end in the same can.*

Nauman's PsalmBook

When genoming opens our ears to inhuman ranges
then noises we now judge *fair as the rose in May*

will sound brittle, then a lilting Chopin *Ballade*
will bring us tidal pain. Instead we will discover

great joy listening to soprano white smoke
float from brick stacks, or from the thespian notes

of a brown spider slinging her webs against glass.
A sand granule abrading a sand grain will bring tears

that slide over your skin like coda to requiem.
In this future, families will gather round the radiator

to hearken to the heaven-plated voices of the dead:
Get away from my tomb! Get out of my head!

The Bowling Pin Forest

The narcotic blue moonlight balms hickory
and slides across the woods' tea meal.

A screech owl calls a hoot owl a bad name.
The autumn rain elides all other moods.

I dance like night writing. I smell syrup
and mashed fruit. I know better than speak.

Each word summons a familiar.
                                    Thirty years

back aiming for a buck my father shot
a hole into a wind maple. With his gummy

knife he carved our initials round the black
shell scoop.

                    I wander our extinguished
scrape looking for that tree. Always I find

the man. I sit on a stone, smoke, feel dead
satisfaction. The owls bandy sophistries.

                        Only the mice escape.

Buzzcocked

Too hot to ideate,
        I rock in my glider
        watching mosquitoes
        squito and stars star as
        a pink belly moon gets
        all Bela and Chaney.

Space junk torrefies.
        I remember you.

As kids we wished
        upon metal fishtailing
        back to earth to resolve
        into beautiful dust
        above my Pop's mutant
        apple orchard field.

You put my hand
        on your breast, twice
        before I understood.

Your dad despised me.

Your mom made me
        read, *Our Bodies, Ourselves*
        and Judy Blume. So,
        women, too, can come
        too soon?

You had a hole
        for chem saturation and
        waltzing the barn floor
        to the Buzzcock's
        effortlessly elegiac
        "Orgasm Addict."

And here you are,
        back from long past.

Heat of wet skin, spunk of gravity.

Shocking.

Sehnsucht

Bald crow holds shapes from his linden like a sachem,
a Bosch stain, strange muse. *I am your rind.* April is
cold, wet—bleak time and fast dusk. I wear coveralls
the color of ripe slime. His tree has not flowered; its fat,
sticky buds have misplayed their blossoming orders.

Last night, I heard a walking bass, hunting bugles and
Moog meringues just below the skull orchard's teeth.
The bird gunkholes the birch forests. Its crown is bare
skull—Cremnitz yarmulke. *I am your sweet bark, rind.*

Agrichines rust in the hung-fired fields. Echo Lake is
humus-stunk, lungmoth brown. The crow comes for me.
I follow through brush, dry scrub, I hear thumping wings,
hooves, *nacht*-laden notes that lead to a pheasant fucked
to shreds by dogs, I hope. I make definitive fire. We eat.

Awfrgawdsakes

The Age of Iron began in order
to produce lovely, deadly weapons.

I flick Sinatra off. Out my window
the sick lawn blues lunar glue.

A thin hare stares daggers at me
from his impossible exile.
                              Do you asleep?

Inside, a wahwah moth pursues an idea
of Yahweh as it pursues me.
                              No?

Outside, the hare (malign strategist)
trades his body

for a used shadow. I wish a hand
would descend touch

my head slide and rub
eyeballs out.
                    Yes? Are you sleep?

The lurky hare rounds up.
Any answer may upset our swarm.

Little one
            the Chairman scats

this number will help us move
from the code of ellipses.

Niagara, Niagara

You may have missed it
　　　　but it's time to depart.

You have very thick paper
　　　　in America, he said.

There are seven names for
　　　　this type of full moon.

I don't remember, will
　　　　you tell me things? she asked.

There are seven names for
　　　　this full moon: peeled onion,

ripe zit, strangled, cataract,
　　　　apoplectic zip, um or laut.

I was trying to extract
　　　　the bones of the matter.

　　　　Emergent worlds must be
curated with a dash of chaos.

We had hopes, she said.
　　　　Blame falls to our dead.

Eskimo Is Lucien

So you say: so this is the cusp, then? My fingers ad-lib
haiku in ASL. It will turn up that I am savant. The stools

are silver flying saucers. The bartender passes us our
pharmacopoeias. Our distance is extenuating, our gerunds

flare like knuckled stars. Over the jukebox Freud warbles,
My brush hairs are tines, watch your Prussian blue eyes.

Our favorite! A sign? You order a Cosmic Trance while
I opt for a Compromised Stanislavski. Neat. "Never seek

spontaneity with a scorecard," you say. I see horns growing
from the driftwood paneled walls. The bartender berates

a rack of elk, he calls this—obtaining an echo. *Let's let our
abdomens exult,* Lucien croons. I turn to say, It's pleasingly

dull—but you are gone, gone, gone. Later I will find your
key on the TV and a note lipstuck to the bedroom mirror:

The Actress must never learn her part aloud. Alone at last
I make my own drinks. I try an Iced Illogical Inspiration,

a Larynx Moondown and a Mortification of Faustus with
lime. On the box, Lucien sings, *So many ears, so few knives.*

Outside, in the tavern's parking lot, two meteorologists
are striking a deal, money is exchanged; it begins to snow.

Walking with Planck

The stars twinkle
     like pix of stars

glacially down-
     loading across

the green screen of
     the Commodore 64.

The cheddar cat
     curls like a snack.

Her front paws hide
     her golden pips.

Her tail sweeps
     the floor for blips.

What Is an Antidote?

How warm is the water?

> In the sea
> by the hotel

> a teenage boy
> masturbates.

How blue is the firmament?

> In the hotel
> under the sea

> the sky cannot
> invert the horizon.

How loud is the tempest?

> In the hotel
> made from seashell

> the echoes
> of every guest

> haunt our
> liver pink halls.

> Sound waves break
> the tortuous walls.

Novemberite

I mean nothing but harm—know that, said the shleepdog
before following a dustbunny back under our bed.

Dik-Dik

All I want in this world
is to face the world
the way the tiny dik-dik—

an odd-nosed antelope
no larger than a fox terrier—

faces off its enemies—
jackal, wild dog, spotted
hyena—with only

its shrill whistle:
Dik-Dik! or *Zik-Zik!*

An eviscerating
agonized scream that
anchors Pendrecki's

Threnody for the Dik-Dik.
All I want. Just that.

Alack

The dimes twinkle
like daystars

in the penny jar
stuck between my

bare bony knees.
How much you

guess you got?
my old man asks.

He doesn't pull
our new Olds into

the empty lot
of the co-op

savings and loan.
I'm almost seven.

Whole lot, I say.
I'll bet, he says,

lighting his pipe.
I'll be here.

Fink

Stories abound as to how Fink received his name. Some trace it to the flow of rum shipments into the cold port of *Beau Fleuve* after Ollie Cromwell's dragon seizure of Jamaica in 1660. Others insist his name refers to his blame in the 1951 basketball point shaving scandal at CCNY. Regardless of his moniker's family tree most agree that Fink's inwit was responsible for ending the belief that silkworms bred in the fingers of the idle virgins of Brookline.

I once heard him at the Pineapple Cotillion: *Why is Jesus so popular with the Ladies?* He spread his oaken arms wide so that his black mourning cloak formed that dread cross. *Because he's hung like this.* When the clapping ceased, it was Tang and bitters all round, all the livelong night. Needless to say none were surprised when he was named ambassador to Saul Bellow. Yes, Fink is genius blessed by seers of social intercourse and the angels of cable threnody.

Not the Kind of Poem Found in the Japanese Edition of *Tiger Beat* or the Ballad of the Bodiless Man

---

After my re*animie*
the first words

I heard?:
Jesus—Help it!

*

You got that
cryo chic

going on,
Mr. Head.

Dr. Pretty Thing
sucks-in her

cheeks, purses
her lips

until they
look fish

and busses
my Petri tank;

once she pressed
her pantyless ass

against my glass.
I swear. Why

would I lie?
Can I lie?

*

I miss toes, nipples,
and sticking

my pinky far
into my ear.

*

*There's elegance in
immobility.*

*Your ghost
is cobalt gouache.*

*

No one proffers
the science of how

they uplink
my brain to quick.

Or, who I am
or who I was.

Criminal? Agent?
Alien? Saint?

Father? Son?
Unholy ghost?

I'm submerged
in this aqua-Velveeta

that gives my hair
a *Wuthering* Heathcliff-

on-the-moors wave.
I liked to wave.

That's how
Dr. PT

puts it, she puts it,
Hey Mr. Head,

how 'bout a smidgen
of Rain eye shadow

Beige? Context
is king.

How 'bout
a beeswax balm?

Don't wanna freak
the monks

when they come
to wonk.

Hero? Fool?
Scientist?

Hopeless Romantic?
Machine?

Lip-gloss? *Text gloss.*
Is this heaven?

*

I miss itching
between my toes

*

Now and then when
I'm not petulant—

when my irritants
have evacuated—

they hotwire my
hippocampus so

I can recall
orgasms

with a blink
of one lid.

*

Under here,
the world

is a sullen
glow. Is this

world? Ship?
Casually decoupled

inner regions?
Where are my

inner regions?
I miss warm milk.

Someday
they say

they'll give
me the choice

to live
or move on.

Live? Move?
To Tahiti

with Gauguin?
Where do I

come from?
What am I?

Where am I
going?

I miss footy pjs,
bellybutton lint,

and cracking
my mother's back.

I begin
to smell numbers.

*

They pump my tank
with binding proteins,

glucocorticoids
and a pint of

Old Granddad.
Then they let

me vid old oaters
to help me

develop a frenetic
disregard

for self-regard.
I've really come

to really love
Gene Atari

and his joystick
Trigger.

*

In that swath
between

living and living
as gray preserve

(what Hindus call
allfuctup)

that flit
of engagement

reserved
for us

between stations
for the word

quietus–
I am effusion-

less. I am
Beta. Space is tape.

Blink. Blink.
Wink. Blink.

*

I miss the blue
ink star

that shot
across my arm.

Alien Immigrant

When you fall
          into the valley,
think of me
          at the Temple
of the Dyslexic
          Dog, lighting
caesura stalks
          for your trek.

I will anoint
          my bits with
a so-so local
          Chardonnay
then Saab into
          the Mystic
Pottery Barn
          and fall into
a Mahatma
          leather sofa
with my bare
          feet upon a
barbiturate blue
          organdy ottoman
and adore
          the framed repro

of Rothko's
>*Black on Grey*
>*Black on Grey*
>*Black on Grey*

until my tears
>stain your way.

Crack

Where are the bridges?

Sometimes the water   silver and oil, sometimes snap green.
Across the river   crow chirrs seep from a pine nevus. They play me

down they say:

Beetles in baroque armor acquit from the milk draw.

I will count words that end in K until I can come awak.

three

Little Poe Station

The whistle of the noon Aniline makes me think of Indian
cinema rain. The air is sheer, unctuous like magazine lotion.

Please: A griseous bone grows over its steel trap.

The inland roads are deserted. The pepper oaks are algebra.
Who has padded the bardo pond with floating terrapin ashtrays?

Attention: Rinse your eyes before you look at us.

The slate sky looks acid buffed and the inflected alkyd light
lets me believe that my feet are not, no, not my own —

Naturally, we have no proof! Tread on principled hope.

I sit under the box, playing with my palm's maze generator.
A bell bells. The gas mask vendor passes me a timetable.

America: Before the Last War

That said, let's remain seated until the credits finish. Look,
this theater was almost empty. We were almost moguls.

The doors are glinting. Which exit did you choose?
God only knows how Johnny Barber, so-called gaffer,

got his union card. He must be someone's nephew.
That said, let's use the remaining minutes to talk about us.

What was it Misty said? In that scene at the bungalow?
Let's get empirical? That's the stub. Let's get empirical.

Who will bear me, the man with the juju hands? Oh,
did you know that Willem Dafoe turned down the part

of Mojo, the fanatical celibate hit-man? He's envisaging.
I'll miss the ambiguous spiccato of your nails against

our empty popcorn box. I'd like to meet someone, I have
an idea for a movie about bookended forethoughts.

It's hard to believe that a filmstrip this vital is only now
receiving its official release. Listen, it sounds like rain,

at dusk, impinging the skin of a Cape cranberry bog.
It sounds like a substitute. I feel like ducking, covering.

Dogs Resembling Their Owners

The evening after the world ends
go to Ahab's for a beer or six.

The jukebox hums the old hymns,
the classics: Autechre, Photek

Joe Aristophanes. No one plugs
new tunes or strews their mask.

Sit among the ones so much like you
it's like you alone. You say shit

nothings so no one pays you
no mind, considers you strange

lonely, satisfied. Some pink cheek
check flush buys a round, low-shelf.

The yellow light glows. *Et tu to you*
the house toasts, *This is our story*

and we're stuck to it. Soon
the amending, soon soon comes

the prayers. Then the pruning shears
and pickle jar are sliding to you—

too late for the wiseass—just
clip a digit (plunk) and pass
                    the drowning on.

Caught between the Twisted Stars

Our coffins catch the ass end of the cortege as it
articulates like a conga line, like a series of snake
like a train-o-wakes. In these vertiginous times
hiring a professional mourner just makes good sense.
I know, check my wallet: *I Carry Card and I Cry Hard.*

After a yard of tears my men and I find a bar where
the bow-tie sporting obit typists can be heard arf-ing
it up with their queer dirges and nicotine sneers
and tactics of denial. Me? I am Kurious George,
your man about deatheatrics in this middling city.

I am the fox brooding the brood. My left eye is posse,
my right one is pack. I am the odd voice whistling
on the breeze. I awake all your comforting verse.
The clock ticks on while I tock your ears off all for
a small fee, salary: a word whose root is salt. See?

Of course when I say coffins I mean a pocket-sized
urn-like, well, urns that we carry in our, well, pockets.
I like to try on the old words. The old terms like:
funereal and bier and battersea and wake and séance
and eulogy and reliquary and cenotaph and RIP.

They remind the customer of former days, days more
or less certain. Or is it more and less uncertain?
Each Thursday afternoon the city lets the streets ooze
with those like us and out we come to dance sweet
tangos with death. I can be your convivial wheeze.

Yes, some find the whole affair obscene, somewhat
ma caw bray. Olé! They're right. Hey, my clients
still download their personalities and memories into
cyber space, outer space onto the Great Hard Drive—
like all, mine too wish to move to ideal permanencies.

Mine just think the world of the world. Mine want
to cover all their equations. See, mine are the kind
that sigh and blush. They take ugly neighbor kids
to frolic in the park. They casually make their points.
They would only pursue from the safety of toy trains.

After the lab coat types are done with their gator clips
and laptops, then my tribe takes charge. We bathe
the body, then rub it up in fragrant, flammable oils.
We wrap them in Egyptian linen and bone the bonfire.
Ash pile to ashes, back to the cave, back to the earth.

Back at the bar there is no discuss of the insoluble situ.
From the old CD jukebox, "Let's Get Dorsal," a classic
Aegeus Saturnhead ballad gurgles. The bongs flow.
I rub my head and one asks, "Checking for your scalp?"
I stand him a beer because he ain't so far from wrong.

Portrait of God on Work Release

I walk to the park
and select a maple leaf.

With my Sharpie I write:
YOU ARE HERE.

Carefully, I return the leaf
to where I found it.

It Ain't Boasting If . . .

My eyelashes
>> are loose sutures.

The teeth
>> reek gasoline.

My fingers?
>> Not handy.

My penis
>> uses mirrors.

Spine
>> recalls its fish.

My toes
>> rattle their chains.

Tongue
>> is flint.

The ears
>> are off at the roots.

My liver has
>> shed its feather.

The belly
>> lullabalizes.

Mandelstam Space Station Down

I hold my breath
to save my mouth.

I am a Jack twitching
outside his box.

Ibids are wading birds
with curved black bills.

You must be loyal
to your nightmares

or they leave you
only dreams, leave

you orbiting above
hard Asian mud.

Klaatu Barada Nikto.
Solemn autumn solemn.

All my enemies have
forgiven me. The bastards.

As the hatch is pried
a klezmer trio plays,

"Now, Cosmonaut,"
accompanied by Her-

who-sings who sings,
"Ibid, ibid, ibid."

The Baudelaire Hospital & Grill

Chiastic Slide

My ashtray fills with peels of green apple. The wallpaper
is Portuguese man-of-war, like cut orange juice. A nurse
tells of SUVs from Jersey still searching Floridas for Disney.

I nod, I too know of the horsehair sails, the Megahertz of
the rave longitudes, midget subs, and Nemo's bottled liver,
kept in the wan lab where they fill our plasma Baggies.

A wax film sky crinkles and scares my resurrectionists, my
sweet fireflies. In the further wards coition screams meld
with the more traditional yawps and yelps. I know I have only

to close my eyes to see small graceful things that I can adore:
an empty Shaker bookcase; kite paper sandals; a Burberry
bush jacket, elbows gone ghost; a raygun silver bagel toaster

shooting infinite slices of black rye across parquet linoleum.
I think swell, so deep, that when I open my eyes my floor
is covered in bread. This is the way it begins. Next the Evian

filled pitchers switch to doggo red. When the shit hits the fan,
it turns to Chanel Christalle. Soon comes the sand, the zombie,
guppies, a nest of apostles, the temple ATM, a backstabber

and a cross. Just thinking about this makes my palms sweat
freaky Fridays. My doctor advises that when these moods strike
I need to pinch my cheek, wink at my mirror and breathe deep.

Pen a pal, she says. Move on, she says. She suggests soup,
masturbation, NASCAR, a week's stay at the Charlie Rose
cetacean clinic in *Via Negativa* with a dash to thoracic Canada.

Confield

In the next bed is a dangerous man—a poet—with a mind-
fucking condition. His hands are secured to his brass cot
with unwaxed floss. Birkenstock clogs have disabled his feet.

His head is covered with a burlap hood. There are holes
for his ear and his mouth. He speaks to me in an uh-oh voice.
He suggests we cut for rum shots. Dare I perturb? See,

what this man writes becomes untrue. It ceases to be, dis-
appears so totally that whatever it was never was. Like he
published a piece in *The New Yorker* notating the motion

of his first lover as she rode (bare-assed) on her pony, Belle
Jar-jar, a pale filly. She passed after a gutsy bout with plunder-
phonia, while the horse, the horse slowly decayed from raw

grief. That poem, those two lines, that heroic couplet, those
twenty syllables squoze tears from a prune. The poet was
praised for his vision, invention and imagination, because

his *elegy* transported the girl and her horse from history to
just poetry. He wrote odes to President Gore, a haiku sequence
on World War III. Is your favorite food Nukeslaw? Made

from Atomic Jackdaw? No! Blame him, that Sphinx that
Cassandra Teiresias! Monster. So he's here as a guest
of our military industrial complex. He asks me again. Cards?

Rum? Then it smacks me, escape? I remove his sack, untie
a hand. I find a pen, paper and whisper my name, my
memoir code. I'll pass him my essential numbers. *Write.*

Envane

Yellow Psalters float across vinegar in the blue flower vase
like baby's first hair. The slats reveal the sun to be Hegelian.
I hear the snow playing Feldman, soft, softest, softer.

When they found me in my room, I had been written into
mystery. No record of me. From the Rimbaud Exercise
Room, off this, the Riding TV Suite, an instructor exhorts,

Sing your name . . . evoke your name! Who is this stranger?
What are you? Where are you? When will you finally see
no one in the barroom mirror but you? Find the grave mask

on your face. Find the mask of your face. This is your life
mask. This is the essential mask that sings your name!
Deepen your voice. Make your voice a noise. Adapt your

body chemically to the impulses that precede that voice,
your noise, that mask, your face, this mirror, sing your
name. Sing your name until you become unrecognizable.

On the screen an ice mummy discusses his tattoos. I am
hungry, but the machine only sells crackerjack prizes.
A conditioner drips water. *Definitely time to move on?*

It's my doctor. *I don't know how you got through our*
security. You tell us and maybe we won't press charges.
Your life must be some fun if you prefer here to there?

By evening I'm free. They give me bus fare into the city
and a Bible black suit. They suggest that I grow a goatee.
My tongue laps the window firefly warm. I taste italics.

Me I Disconnect from You

While searching for drawer pulls to match
my new teeth my Biomimic says, "Animals
that hatch eggs suffer bellybutton envy."

I move my head as a way to convey full
understanding.
        Subdued floor massagers
perform pro in this lively public space—
I feel like I'm floating.
        "Nothing
can replace the intimacy between
an object and its human."
        The gracious
loam, supported by microclimating, transforms
the mall into the end, the product itself.

Stately Europeans sweat to Yo-Yo Ma.

"Fingers will not only survive but remain
the instrument of choice for doodlers."

I suggest a time-out at the martini hut.

"Let us be lovers and marry our Warhols
together," it sings.
        I order again
and suggest that it's its turn to wear the skin.

"Put my sensor flats over your ears, you'll
swear you hear the ancient inland sea."
        I

order again.

Earth Is a Lonely Town

Just when things
got so eloquent

so mad that *we*
was a sobriquet

for *grand* she
went and said *this* . . .

*us . . . just, can't
go on . . . see, my world*

*is too big to
include you.*

That's the way she
spoke. An ellipsist.

Perhaps it was common
to her planet.

Hesitations, pauses,
a mumble or two

then boom . . . a kiss
on the lips or

a sock to
the solar plexus.

There was copious
medicine in that

silence. After living
with so many

periods, commas
the effect and affect

of her alien
drama dragged me

into the loop
of her orbit.

I think she feared
reentry. There might

be someone
scary there, a station

that meant more than
dot to dot.

But that's me being
wishy as she saw

death in the pauses
where I saw. . . .

She left me here, left
in her old rocket.

She had another vision
wrapped around her head

and she mentioned . . .
deadlines and mission

creep and said her world
was too big for me.

It shouldn't matter now,
could be relative,

except . . . I think I . . . still. . . .

And though this happened
millennia ago

the memory of her skin,
her speech, is seed

deeper than my own
bones. It's hard

not to rot a bit,
to simply, simply

just exist, to get
your kicks pricking

existential violets.
I guess it's

not love when
it's unrequited

but something dark,
darker, stranger,

a cell sealed by
walls, labs of night

where I begin,
again to math

the mess of dust
of stars into

ones and zeros and ones

into chalk lines
that point to her

planet so far so
small, from here.

Architecture and Morality

Our city is a modern city.   Our city
isn't a city in the light   that is given

        to this word today.   It could be
        defined as a kind of   architecture

of impatience   with a faint
hint of humanity−   lurking under

        our trapeziums   −that softens
        the dark backgrounds   in the way

open windows do.   Move to
our pristine center   square; past

        the scene's subject   is the past:
        a silent train   smoke rising

like signals   into linearity:
into sky   cloudless sky.

Nosing

A raven carries a scarecrow's bones across the river, to a glaring at
the edge of a winter day. The caw factory shifts from *ololuge*, the cry
of joy at a sacrifice when the offering is struck to the *kokutos*, the dirge.
At the edge of town we are building a moor to hold our new stories.

Nosology

From *A List of Known Diseases* (2039): colloquy, bootleg, Xerox sleeve,
the unseensies, ether talk, misbehavings, death, and download pox.

Nostalgia

It's one of those days I guess, like in a Russian novel or a Polish curse
or a Chinese poem where rain is rain and a fat cat sips your ice cream.

Nostoc

An emanation from the stars. A tricky question. First found
in rural Tango on the Japanese coast. Earth is a lonely town. When
he left home in the morning to attend the School his mother struck
two flints together. We will incorporate that noise into your dream.

Nostradamus

It's one of those days, I guess. I self-identify as a non-ideological
ideologue like, I think that zoos are nicer on gray days, like that.

Nostril

Dawn flashes like a toothbrush wound. After pouring and chanting
we take our seats in the ditch. Children appear and can even sing.

Nostrum

A pet scheme, a quack remedy, a cabal in your medicine closet;
Zapruderista!: one who has mastered the art of murder by amnesia.
One morning you appear for brunch and your signifier says: who
are you? Then the others say, to him: to whom are you speaking?

Not

"And sometimes not. My wife and I are having a baby. She's pregnant,
at the moment. And they've just done this test that claims that its

Nota Bene

chances, our baby's chances of getting Down's syndrome have risen
from one in 3200 to one in 3100. Algorithms. They advise more zinc."

Notability

Abruptly the needy birds get fitful. The trees follow suit. Cones
are dropping like flies. One is reminded of Aeschylus's *Agamemnon*
when the chorus can hear the king braying bloody murder as he is
bloodily murdered. They speak about what to do. They do nothing.

Notable

On their first restaurant date, he told her, "I am contradiction tolerant."
He ordered his steak, "Notable." She drank more than was her wont.

Notandum

She called her diary MY GENETIC BACKGROUND. For 12/17/09:
My labor selection will be noted then promoted as consumer choice.

Notarial

From *A List of Known Diseases* (1939): an anthropologist in Maine,
down in Maine? Up in Maine? He had one ear. He was, on balance,
unbalanced. He and his son were putting a roof on the son's house.
The father's shingles were crossed and split. The father's nails

Notary

were bent. The son got upset and pushed his father off his roof,
to his death. The chorus spoke about what to do. They did nothing.

Notation

Zapruderista! slogans: Machine your abeyance! Egg your chicken!
Plausible skin! Aesthetic rogues steal our codes! Claustrophobism!

Not-Being

There's a funny anecdote about Hegel. Somewhere. There must be.
Stories with Hegel, gas, and close quarters on the Orient Express?
Or maybe he goes to see Barnum's circus and is volunteered to be
the magician's assistant. Something with a box that ends in poof!

Notch

He fit the arrow to the bowstring. Before he could release, the air
pullulated with crow. His fingers turned to straw. The doe ran free.

Notching

The chorus gathered like a jury in the room of their peer. Poof!
The Zapruderista! have *All and / or Nothing* on film. Egg your chickens!

Note

In rich fortunes we will labor. Our seasons pass in cellophane
wraps. In a copse spangled with myrtle, our hydrant-sniffing dogs
are run through their drills. Lets' Bijou. Let's wave to our barber,
spinning in his chair like a centrifuge until the whole town sees stars.

Finally We Are No One

No zeitgeist
　　　goes unhectored,

the Professor
　　　lectures our class.

I will take
　　　an in-your-face

approach to
　　　analyzing

our historic
　　　broach with Them.

Through the blue
　　　window

I train my eye
　　　on our people

wheeling-in
　　　a new missile,

shaped like a
　　　Popsicle.

Or is it
　　　a space engine?

Two by two
      we will walk,

I think, the black-
      board

is a perfect
      fond for stars.

Inhaler

Watson-

I open my mouth
to let your ash enter.

-Crick

I open my mouth—
smoke rushes out.

THE IOWA POETRY PRIZE & EDWIN FORD PIPER POETRY AWARD WINNERS

1987

Elton Glaser, *Tropical Depressions*

Michael Pettit, *Cardinal Points*

1988

Bill Knott, *Outremer*

Mary Ruefle, *The Adamant*

1989

Conrad Hilberry, *Sorting the Smoke*

Terese Svoboda, *Laughing Africa*

1990

Philip Dacey, *Night Shift at the Crucifix Factory*

Lynda Hull, *Star Ledger*

1991

Greg Pape, *Sunflower Facing the Sun*

Walter Pavlich, *Running near the End of the World*

1992

Lola Haskins, *Hunger*

Katherine Soniat, *A Shared Life*

1993

Tom Andrews, *The Hemophiliac's Motorcycle*

Michael Heffernan, *Love's Answer*

John Wood, *In Primary Light*

1994

James McKean, *Tree of Heaven*

Bin Ramke, *Massacre of the Innocents*

Ed Roberson, *Voices Cast Out to Talk Us In*

1995

Ralph Burns, *Swamp Candles*

Maureen Seaton, *Furious Cooking*

1996

Pamela Alexander, *Inland*

Gary Gildner, *The Bunker in the Parsley Fields*

John Wood, *The Gates of the Elect Kingdom*

1997

Brendan Galvin, *Hotel Malabar*

Leslie Ullman, *Slow Work through Sand*

1998

Kathleen Peirce, *The Oval Hour*

Bin Ramke, *Wake*

Cole Swensen, *Try*

1999

Larissa Szporluk, *Isolato*

Liz Waldner, *A Point Is That Which Has No Part*

2000

Mary Leader, *The Penultimate Suitor*

2001

Joanna Goodman, *Trace of One*

Karen Volkman, *Spar*

2002

Lesle Lewis, *Small Boat*

Peter Jay Shippy, *Thieves' Latin*